Postcards From The Hedge

A Bestiary of the Night

First published 2019 by The Hedgehog Poetry Press

Published in the UK by
The Hedgehog Poetry Press
5, Coppack House
Churchill Avenue
Clevedon
BS21 6QW

www.hedgehogpress.co.uk

ISBN: 978-1-9160908-7-3

Copyright © Mark Davidson 2019

The right of Mark Davidson to be identified as the editor of this work has been asserted in accordance with the Copyright, Designs and Patents Act 1988. All rights for individual works retained by the respective author.

All rights reserved. No part of this publication may be reproduced, stored in or introduced into a retrieval system, or transmitted in any form, or by any means (electronic, mechanical, photocopying, recording or otherwise) without prior written permissions of the publisher. Any person who does any unauthorised act in relation to this publication may be liable for criminal prosecution and civil claims for damages,

9 8 7 6 5 4 3 2 1

A CIP Catalogue record for this book is available from the British Library.

Do you remember closing your eyes to go to sleep only for your overactive imagination to take control and turn every shadow into a monster, every squeak of a floorboard into the footsteps of some strange and scary animal, every breath tasting of magic and mystery and no matter how tightly you squeezed your eyes shut, you knew not to open them?

We have news for you.

Something really was watching you.

Poetry From...

Desmond Childs 7
Val Ormrod 8
Pratibha Castle 10
Anna Teresa Slater 11
Ceinwen E. Cariad Haydon 12
Nick Toczek 14
Genya Johnson 15
Simon Buckland 16
Anne Casey 18
Darren J Beaney 20
Karren Middleton 21

DESMOND CHILDS

Bedlam

How you cling
to the roof of my mind
That esoteric creature
Of folded wings;
and hueless eyes;
of quiet gaze: resounding

That creature of dream
Of unfurling wings
Of torment of mind and;
angst of night
of stretch of skin:
flit of shadow; in candlelight

With bead of eye; and
beat of wings; bedlam
through the night you bring
Like moths intrigue
Amour of flame
I'm draw into; your
resounding gaze

VAL ORMROD

Footsteps

Lying rigid in the dark throat of night,
breath shallow, blood chilled,
eyes focused and still.

I am a rock, a tree, a tightly-folded flower,
a cactus. I am the cold moon,
watching and waiting

for the slow turning of the door knob,
the soft pad of feet drawing closer.
I am a drum. I beat wildly.

Eyes screwed shut, I curl inwards,
sinews taut. I am chalk
screaming across a blackboard.

Footsteps pause. Breath held.
Bedcover quivers with a chill rush of air.
Fingers trespass.

I am a green fig, an unripe peach,
the stone amid a cherry
sliced through and prised apart.

My small hands clasped,
guided to the target.
The world flares red.

I am seared, I am scalded,
I am spinning in fire.
I am a violin screeching out of tune.

I am a willow, bowed and weeping.
I am a songbird without song,
lying limp in the dark bowel of night,

no longer watching, but waiting –
for the slow turning of the door knob,
the soft pad of feet to grow faint.

PRATIBHA CASTLE

Vulture Crone

Toys cavalcade across the fence.

Spider Man frisbee in Union
Jack colours, venom green
boomerang grudging on return,
rugby ball padded like a cell.

In the bomb site of her garden
she laments her beloved rose,
a *Cecile de Mille* extravaganza,
magenta diva face smashed

by hooligan disdain, broke
necked in company with the punk
calendula, truss of *Tumbling
Tom* till yesterday so fey.

Flicker book slick, a seed
in seconds morphing to a tree,
she sprouts a universe of curves.
The wicked witch of fables,

vulture crone, fingers
gnarled to dragon knuckles,
spine stooped, crook chin
reaching up to nutcracker nose,

warts on its bulbous tip
like woodland fungi
or a dead blood
jelly baby. Voice

abrading to a bullfrog croak,
incantations spuming from her lips.

ANNA TERESA SLATER

The Girl and Her Battles

As long as I stayed within the frame of my bed, I was safe.
The Night Claw, I suppose, didn't like little girl limbs
straying beyond spaces assigned for human slumber.
I buried myself in the center, pillows fortified all sides,
tucked in my nose, curled my toes into creeping commas,
mimicked a reluctant corpse parked in a cocoon.

Interesting how I rarely cared for humour in the dark,
how I assumed the Night Claw would take revenge
on any under cover giggle or display of faux pluck.
Every edge was enemy, each corner a red zone.
My bladder: that treacherous friend! That sneaky foe!
No, 12 a.m. left zero room for laughter or play for this girl.

The Night Claw still makes itself felt even in my late years.
But now I dare it to appear and I hang my arms and legs
past borders into the black, still air. I anticipate the grab,
the pierce, my mid-aged shriek. But all there is is silence.
All there is is the moon moving through the sky as I sleep,
and the sun coming up, and the day that needs living.

CEINWEN E. CARIAD HAYDON

after seven o'clock

some nights   bad bedtimes
hid behind billowed curtains
sleep's safety
snatched its arms from me

abandoned   alone
scared   on tense toes
I crept downstairs
encountered another demon
squat on our mantlepiece

its tick-tock workings
choked my throat   its hands'
relentless circling
wrung tears from infant eyes –

its cold round face stared
and threatened my demise
it fed my mortal dread
of late hours   of adult time
after I'd been sent to bed

if mummy was elsewhere   busy
and daddy was feeling kind
he'd turn its numbers toward the wall
and calm me down again

if mummy was cross and crazy
as she very often was   she'd yank me
back to my darkened room   chide me
you naughty girl   words spat out
through hisses of bad breath

she'd tell me   stay asleep   don't stir
or I'd very soon be sorry
very soon be dead

NICK TOCZEK

Hungry

From the dark primeval depths
Of the lake that workmen dredge

Something slippery slithers
To the surface, to the edge,

Some strange freak of evolution
Oozing over reeds and sedge.

Something sluggish slides tonight
Smoothly through the moonless hedge.

Something sticky, thick and viscous
Sludges past the blooms and veg.

Something slimy's slowly climbing
Onto the open window-ledge...

GENYA JOHNSON

The Girl With The Shawl

How could I ever forget that night?
Icy cold room
Breath billowing
Into nothingness
As fingers and feet
Numb with cold
Couldn't find warmth under
The eiderdown

I wanted to open my eyes
Yet I wanted them to remain
Tightly closed as
The unexpected
The unexplained
The unknown
Was waiting for me

Was she there, the girl with the
White shawl covering her shoulders
Hair, dark and long
Hanging over her shoulders
Eyes, piercing into the darkness
Face, pure white like a porcelain doll
Standing at the side of my bed
Watching me

Did I scream?
Did I throw the blankets
Over my head?
Did I look again
The room was icy cold
When I opened my eyes
But all I saw was another's breath billowing
Onto my pillow.

SIMON BUCKLAND

Supersaver off-peak getaway

Into the station whoof-whoofled the train –
      chip-shop, chip-shop, chop-ship.
Showering us all with great clouds of fireflies
      which nibbled and niggled and nipped.

Jerky white clouds were scudding in front of
a jolly old sun on a stick.
A stiff little breeze brushed the piano-key trees –
      hip-hop, hip-hop, hop-hip.

With a squawk of the brakes and a groan from the engine,
      the train dragged itself to a halt.
And then the doors were bam-clam-slattered open
      as the passengers all tumbled out.

There were white geese and ducks in sensible bonnets
tied neatly up under their beaks,
There were frogs and tortoises in bright yellow waistcoats,
while foxes and badgers breathed beer and tobacco,
with racing tips stuffed in their breeks.

In a hackle and clutter they all left the station,
      and no one was left there – save me.
The battered old engine was thumping and gasping
      and all of the doors of all the compartments
      were open – save one.

The sun had gone orange, burnt crisp round the edges,
with a seaweed moustache and deep lines in his forehead,
he turned up the heat by degrees.

And that last door inched open,
        ever-ever-ever-so-slowly,
And I walked up the platform, feeling sicker and heavier
        and the thing that was inside began to creep outside
        as its limbs began to appear,
        like dusty old fragments of broken umbrellas,
                it creaked and it hissed, and it rustled and rattled,
Till all of it finally stood on the platform
        and then started reaching for me.

Arm-in-leg, leg-in-arm, we edged down the platform,
        and into the streets of the town.
        It breathed like a bellows,
        tip-tapped on the pavement,
while I hummed 'My Sweet Lord' and played with a conker
        using my free hand, so the thing wouldn't see me,
so that I might hang onto my soul.

Now the sky was the colour of gravy,
        as the sun turned asparagus green.
With a jagged blue scar on his forehead,
        he sneered and he scowled at the scene.

And the angles were all going crooked,
        the streets folded in on themselves,
The streetlamps flowed into the pavements,
and there rose up a foul yellow smell,

Then all of a sudden I was under and inside,
        in darkness like blindness,
and the thing was contracting,
squeezing tighter and tighter,
        getting more and more breathless,
and all I remember
is this.

ANNE CASEY

Watching and waiting

If you listen carefully   you can hear them
whispering amongst themselves   about us   and how we   came to be

I found one   in our garage once   almost luminous white   with the faintest hint
of ghostly green   lurking behind a cardboard box   of forgotten important things

It had made its way   from the far end   of the garden
all the way under the house   and up through   the concrete floor

sitting there in the semi-dark   all fragile and inert   unless you strained   right up clo
to those anaemic waxy tendrils   the fine white hairs   vibrating with the creed:

"Long, long ago when Mother Earth was free—
Before the first Human was made, all the Trees lived in harmony
With every Creature under Father Sky. All the world existed in perfect balance—

But one day Small Grey Rabbit stopped to graze
Near Mountain Stream. Weeping Willow watched Small Grey Rabbit
Bounding about, her tiny feet free to take her wherever her little heart pleased.

Weeping Willow shook with jealous desire
To pull his feet from the restraining soil. A branch broke off and fell to Earth—
Crushing Small Grey Rabbit—her blood staining the soil at Weeping Willow's feet.

Willow greedily drank the spilled blood.
Father Sky darkened and Great Wind blew, uprooting Weeping Willow
With a mighty screech that foretold Willow would forevermore walk on two legs;

All his children would be born from blood;
They would no longer be nourished by Father Sky
Or nestle in Mother Earth's warm embrace. From that day forward,

Willow and his progeny were condemned
To roam the earth, struggling to survive—until
They had returned every last drop of plundered blood."

If you listen carefully   you can hear them
whispering amongst themselves   about us   and how we'll   meet our end

That's right   the trees have our number
peering in a window   scratching at a roof   they understand

justice is a waiting game

DARREN J BEANEY

Afraid of the dark

Mother never got it. An icepack
on my brow was certainly not going
to comfort. Cooling was not an answer.

I yearned for parental protection. Needed mum
to be a beehive Boudica, commanding her swinging
warrior hordes to guard my door. To clothe
dad in a sixties style suit of shining armour,
to instruct him to fight my nocturnal antagonists.

I wanted my young folks to play distracting games,
0's & X's, corrective battleships
and remedy destroyers. Simple frolics
to close my thinking to the stirring drapes,
that created a surly canopy, always stretching
to tear at my tender toes. I begged my parents

to recite amusing tales to stifle the menacing chatter
of malignant magpies nesting in my pillows,
always attempting to abduct my slumber. I often
requested that my mama or papa
should sing sweet lullabies to drown the chants
of massed risky monks whose dancing shadows
were in the habit of scaring. I hoped a show

of warmth from mummy and daddy would make
the devilish stuntmen crash and burn as they double dared
me to risk it all and try this at home. I knew if mom
tucked me in, tight, all the accident-prone muted monsters,
who thrived on long winter nights, would just scuttle
off into misfortune. If ma wished me sweet dreams
I understood my dreams would be full of colour,
not transparent terror. But most of all

I wished my brave mum and dad would just to leave the light on.

KARREN MIDDLETON

I Open My mouth, But No Screams Come Out!

They say your life flashes before your eyes just before you die
Then why can't I bring a thought to mind, why?
My dressing gown on the back of the bedroom door
Has grown hands and reaches down and tries the handle of the door?
I open my mouth, but no screams come out.

Why must I wrap my sweaty clammy, hands, around my book, tight?
Without a doubt, dressing gown by day monster by night
I open my mouth, but no screams come out.

In the place of the wardrobe door,
Stands a wooden man I haven't noticed before,
All dressed in black with a
Wooden lion and a wooden witch on his back.
They keep switching places, so I don't know which is witch,
Or which side the lion's face is,
I open my mouth, but no screams come out.

In my lampshade lives a weirdy beardy man,
I don't know how much more I can take,
My breath does a sharp intake.
I open my but no screams come out.

The darkness so loud, the frightness, so close I can touch
My eyes continue to play tricks on me so much
Shadows pick my wall, my drawer and discarded book,
And make a, I'm coming to get you look.
I don't wanna feel the way I'm feeling
I don't wanna see the sights I'm seeing,
I don't wanna hear the sounds of steps nearing
And I don't wanna hear the floorboards creaking.

But sometimes sound of silences ring in my head
I want to sleep I want to go to bed

Why do I open my mouth, but no screams come out?

www.ingramcontent.com/pod-product-compliance
Lightning Source LLC
Chambersburg PA
CBHW021135080526
44587CB00012B/1303